SAVE THAT TRASH!

Written by Maryann Dobeck
Illustrated by Meryl Henderson

Save that trash.

Don't toss it out.

Make something from it.

3

Save that trash.

Make a flowerpot.

1. Make sure it is clean.

2. Add dirt.

3. Plant some seeds.

4. Place the flowerpot in the sun.

5

Save that trash.

Make a bag puppet.

1. Make sure it is clean.

2. Tape on things to make a face.

3. Tape on other things you like.

4. Make the puppet move.

Save that trash.

Make a drum.

1. Make sure it is clean.

2. Put the top back on.

3. Paste on what you like.

4. Tap the drum.

Save that trash.

Make a bird feeder.

1. Make sure it is clean.

2. Tape it on a hanger.

3. Add food for birds.

4. Hang the bird feeder in a good place.

Save that trash.

Make a vase.

1. Make sure it is clean.

2. Tape on what you like.

3. Add some water.

4. Put some flowers in the vase.

Save that trash.

Make a caterpillar.

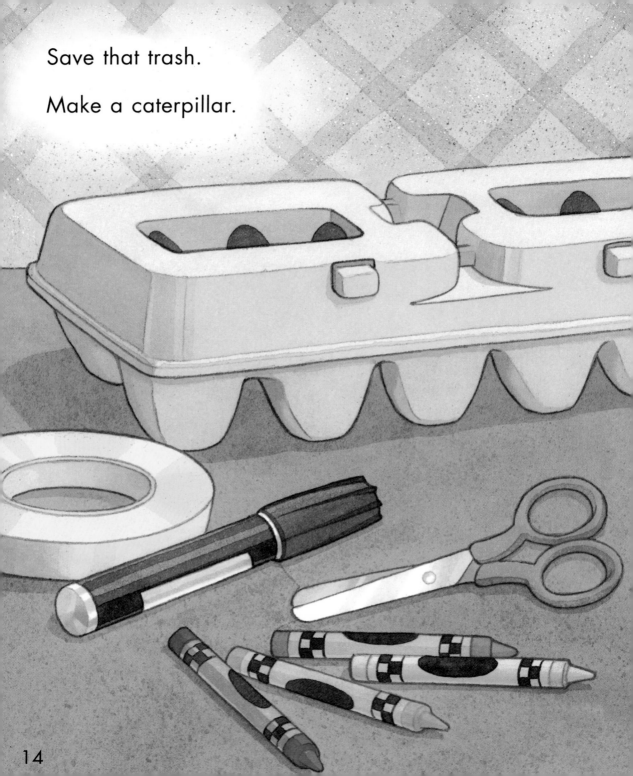

1. Make sure it is clean.

2. Cut it apart. Tape it together.

3. Make a face at one end.

4. Hold the caterpillar and make it crawl.

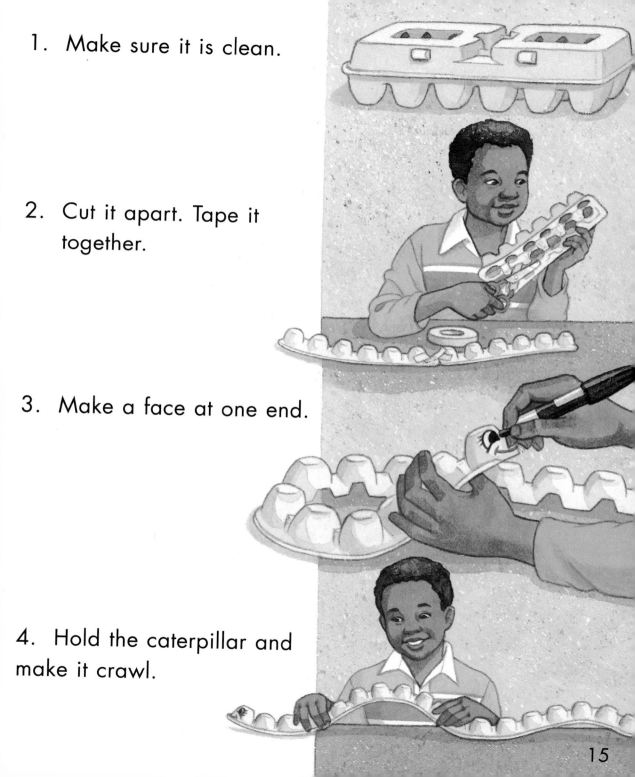

Save that trash.

Don't throw it out.

Make something from it.